21st Century Skills **INNOVATION LIBRARY**

EMERGING Tech

Robots

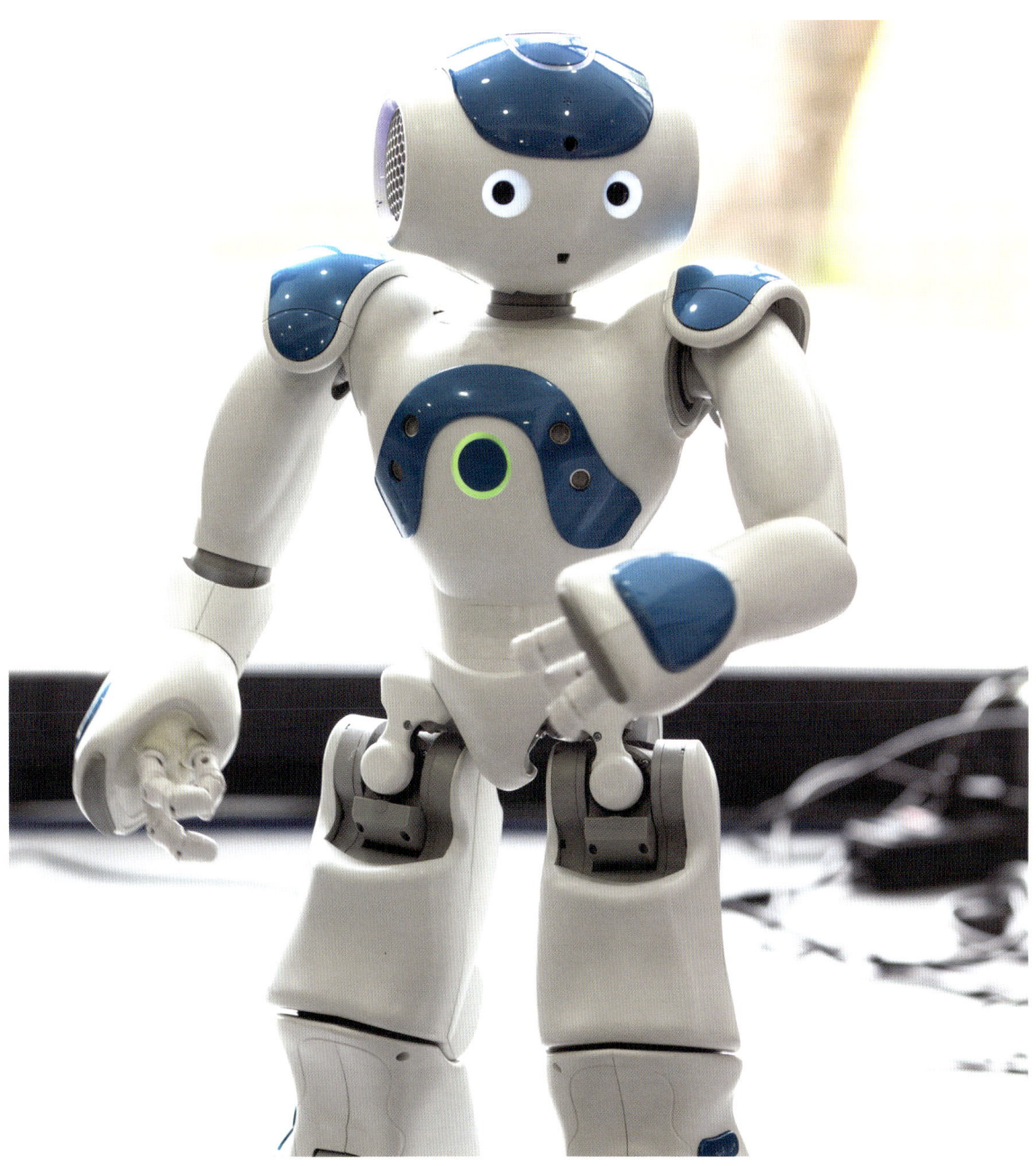

CHERRY LAKE PUBLISHING • ANN ARBOR, MICHIGAN

by Josh Gregory

A Note to Adults: Please review the instructions for the activities in this book before allowing children to do them. Be sure to help them with any activities you do not think they can safely complete on their own.

A Note to Kids: Be sure to ask an adult for help with these activities when you need it. Always put your safety first!

Published in the United States of America by Cherry Lake Publishing
Ann Arbor, Michigan
www.cherrylakepublishing.com

Content Editor: Matthew Lammi, Assistant Professor of Technology, Engineering & Design Education, North Carolina State University
Reading Adviser: Marla Conn MS, Ed., Literacy Specialist, Read-Ability, Inc.
Photo Credits: Cover and page 1, ©Cylonphoto/Shutterstock; page 4, ©Sarunyu L/Shutterstock; page 7, ©Nataliya Hora/Shutterstock; page 9, ©DenisKlimov/Shutterstock; page 10, NASA/JPL-Caltech/MSSS; page 13, ©Lerner Vadim/Shutterstock; page 14, ©Aurora Photos/Alamy Stock Photo; page 15, ©Master Video/Shutterstock; page 16, ©Ned Snowman/Shutterstock; page 18, ©Sergei Tremasov/Shutterstock; page 19, ©designelements/Shutterstock; pages 21 and 24, ©REUTERS/Alamy Stock Photo; page 22, ©AlesiaKan/Shutterstock; pages 25 and 27, ©dpa picture alliance/Alamy Stock Photo; page 28, ©Xinhua/Alamy Stock Photo

Copyright ©2018 by Cherry Lake Publishing
All rights reserved. No part of this book may be reproduced or utilized in
any form or by any means without written permission from the publisher.

Library of Congress Cataloging-in-Publication Data has been filed and is available at catalog.loc.gov

Cherry Lake Publishing would like to acknowledge the work of the Partnership for
21st Century Learning. Please visit *www.p21.org* for more information.

Printed in the United States of America
Corporate Graphics

21st Century Skills INNOVATION LIBRARY

Contents

Chapter 1	**A Long History**	4
Chapter 2	**On the Job**	10
Chapter 3	**At Home and in the Classroom**	18
Chapter 4	**The Future of Robots**	24

Glossary	30
Find Out More	31
Index	32
About the Author	32

EMERGING TECH

Chapter 1

A Long History

When you hear the word *robot*, what comes to mind? Maybe you think of a movie like *Star Wars*, where robot characters play important roles as heroes and villains. Or maybe there are robots in your favorite video games or comic books. Or maybe your first thought isn't of a story at all. Maybe it's of a robot that you see every day in your own home!

For a very long time, robots existed mostly in people's imaginations. The idea of a machine that could move and think without being directly controlled by a

For the movie *Star Wars: The Force Awakens*, engineers built a real, working robot to play the character of BB-8.

human operator was considered science fiction. Some forward-thinking inventors sketched out designs and even built robot-like machines. But even they couldn't have imagined the variety of incredible robots that exist today. Some are tiny, while others are enormous. Some look a lot like people or animals, but many don't look like anything else you've ever seen before. They often are used to complete important jobs. But there are also many robots that were built just for fun!

What exactly makes something a robot? After all, many of the electronic devices people use today are able to think for themselves. Some of them can even carry on conversations with users. However, a computer or a smartphone is not the same thing as a robot. A robot is a mechanical device that has the ability to move around in some way. Robots often have motors, arms, legs, or wheels. Some can grab things the way hands do. Others have faces that can move to form humanlike facial expressions. Some can walk or drive around, while others are stuck in one place.

Robots must also be able to operate without humans controlling them. This means they must have a computerized "brain" that can be programmed. The simplest robots are programmed to complete the

EMERGING TECH

Machines with Minds of Their Own

The study of artificial intelligence will play a big role in building smarter, more humanlike robots. Modern robots can be programmed to absorb a lot of information and make complicated decisions, but they cannot think for themselves and solve problems the way humans can. If a robot comes into a situation it isn't programmed to handle, it won't know what to do. It cannot learn new things or come up with ideas on its own.

Scientists are hoping to change this in the future. They want to create robots that can learn new things and adjust their own programming as needed to solve problems. This would make them very similar to humans!

same action over and over again. They do their job the same way every time. You might see these kinds of robots in factories. For example, a factory robot might be programmed to attach a certain piece to a car. After it is done, the car is moved along to another robot, which attaches a different piece.

Other robots are a little bit smarter. They might be programmed to observe their surroundings using a variety of **sensors**. For example, such robots might be able to detect motion, light, or temperature. The instructions programmed into their computer brains tell them how to react when their sensors detect certain changes in the environment. For instance, maybe a security robot is programmed to patrol an office building at night. If its sensors detect motion, it can investigate to see if an intruder is nearby.

The smartest robots are able to make split-second decisions and respond to an incredible number of situations, much like people or animals. No matter how smart a robot is, however, it can only do what its creators have programmed it to do. The scientists and **engineers** who are pushing robot technology forward today are building on a long history of knowledge gained from other innovators.

Robotic arms assemble the pieces of a car at a factory.

EMERGING TECH

As far back as the third century BCE, inventors in ancient China created robot-like machines called automatons. These were mechanical devices that moved around in entertaining ways. For example, a bird-shaped automaton might flap its wings. An automaton shaped like a band played music. Automatons were built using a variety of materials and were powered using water, wind, and other sources.

Over the following centuries, inventors around the world created better and better automatons. While these devices weren't very useful beyond entertainment, they helped lead to further robotic developments.

As technology improved, writers and storytellers began to imagine a world where we lived alongside robots that looked and behaved just like people. In 1921, writer Karel Capek coined the term *robot* in a play about such **humanoid** machines. Since then, we have used this word to refer to many kinds of automated machines.

In the 20th century, inventors began to see the potential for automated machines to perform tasks in place of human workers. During the 1960s, inventor George Devol designed and built a robotic arm called the Unimate. This groundbreaking creation changed

ASIMO waves to the crowd at a demonstration in 2008.

the world of robotics forever. In 1961, General Motors began using the Unimate to assemble cars in one of its factories. This made Unimate the first industrial robot to go to work doing a job that once required human workers.

Since then, robot technology has come a long way. Some robot creators have even worked to bring the sci-fi dream of walking, talking humanoid robots into reality. One major breakthrough came with the introduction of Honda's ASIMO robot in 2000. The two-legged, two-armed robot can walk, run, jump, and even play soccer. It can also carry on simple conversations and recognize physical gestures such as offering it a handshake. With such amazing technology already available, the future of robots could be truly remarkable.

EMERGING TECH

Chapter 2

On the Job

One of the most common places you'll find robots today is at work in many of the same jobs that humans used to perform. Sometimes this is because robots are able to do jobs that are dangerous for humans to perform. Other times, robots are simply more **efficient** than humans at completing certain tasks. They can lift heavy loads and move very quickly. They also don't get tired and rarely make

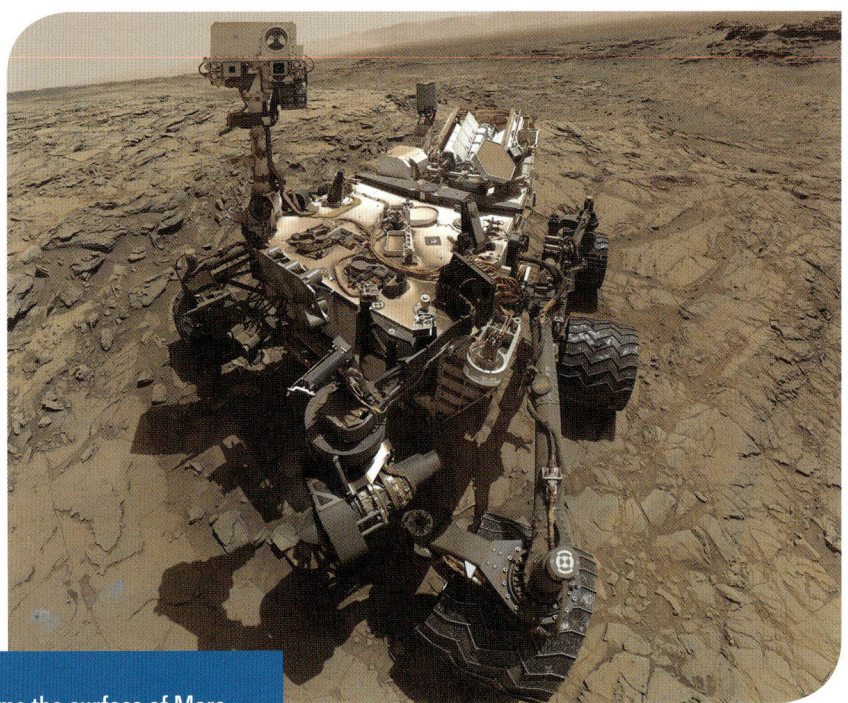

NASA's Curiosity rover roams the surface of Mars.

mistakes. As a result, many manufacturing businesses are always looking for new ways to include robots in their factories.

Today's most interesting robots can do a lot more than just factory work, though. Some of them are helping us explore new worlds. In the early 1970s, the Soviet Union began sending robotic vehicles called rovers to the surface of the moon. Since then, rovers have been an important part of space exploration. They have even visited the surface of Mars. Rovers are sent into space using rockets. Once they land, they can use cameras to take photos. They are also equipped with sensors to collect data about the air, weather, and soil. They can even collect samples of soil and rocks for scientists to study later.

Outer space isn't the only place robots help explore. **Autonomous** underwater vehicles are robots that dive below the surface of the ocean to collect a variety of data. They help researchers hunt for wrecked ships or underwater obstacles such as huge rocks.

Have you ever wondered what the inside of a volcano looks like? Because they are so dangerous

EMERGING TECH

Designing and Building a New Robot

Even with the incredible tools, materials, and other technology available to inventors today, creating a new robot can be difficult. It is a long process that often involves many inventors, each with their own specialties. It all starts with an idea for a way a robot could solve a problem. Inventors then sketch out possible ideas for how the robot could work. They might run computer **simulations** to see if their ideas will work in real life. Then they build a **prototype** of their robot. They test the prototype in different situations and make changes as needed. This process might take many years. The creators might construct countless new prototype versions, with each one improving on the last. Eventually, they settle on a final version to release to the world. But even then, their work isn't necessarily done. They might keep searching for new ways to improve their creation so they can release new versions.

to explore, it was once very hard for humans to study these incredible landforms. However, robot technology is making it easier than ever to crawl into the depths of active volcanoes. Volcano-exploration robots are designed to climb down steep, narrow tunnels as they collect data. Some have many legs, like spiders, while others rely on wheels. They can create maps of the volcano's interior tunnels and collect other information about the environment.

Robots also play important roles in many of today's military and law enforcement operations. One

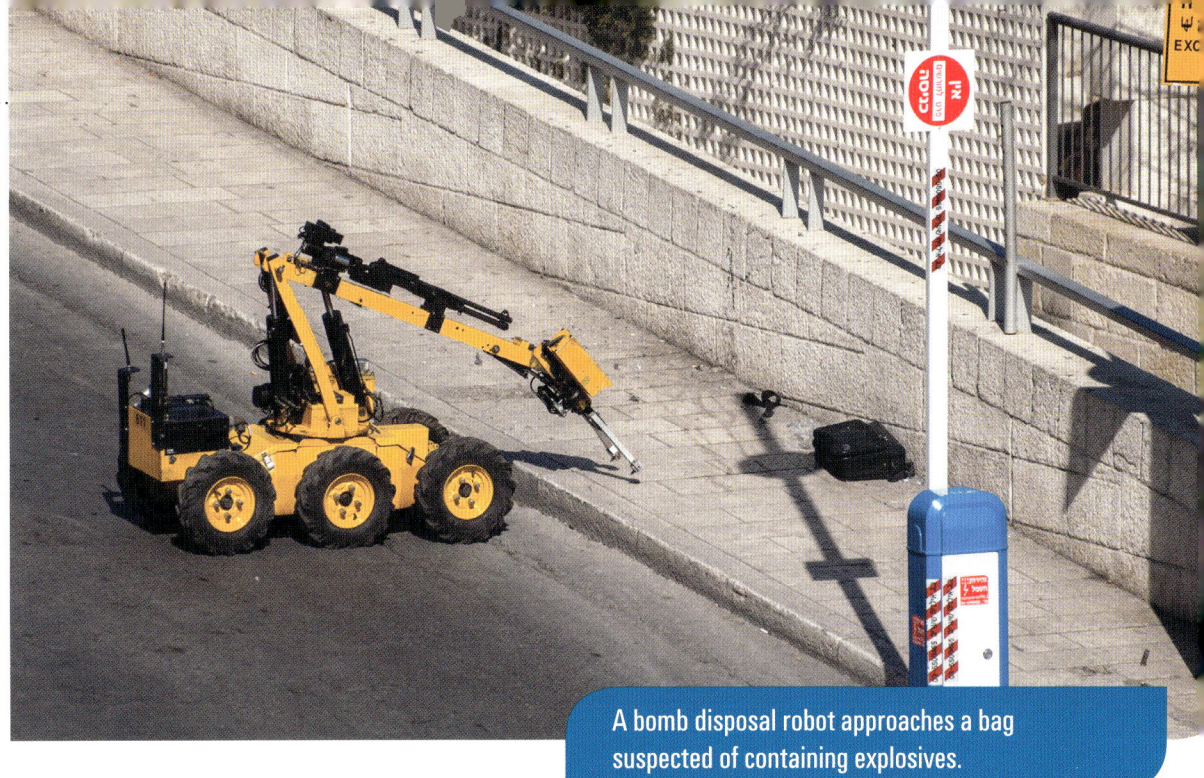

A bomb disposal robot approaches a bag suspected of containing explosives.

especially helpful thing they can do is detect and disarm explosive devices. For example, militaries sometimes plant explosives called land mines underground. When something moves over the top of one of these devices, it will explode. This is a danger not only to soldiers but also many civilians. Worse, these mines often remain buried after wars are over, leaving people who live nearby in danger. They are hard to find and dig up. However, today's robots can use metal detectors to find hidden land mines. This makes it easier for experts to dig them up without getting hurt. There is even an armored robot that can dig up land mines and "eat" them without causing harm to anyone nearby.

EMERGING TECH

Scientists test a robot designed to climb over rubble and other uneven surfaces.

Robots can provide a lot of help when disaster strikes. Earthquakes, hurricanes, and other natural disasters can leave people trapped inside of crumbling buildings or under piles of rubble. It can be hard for rescue workers to locate these people. Even if they do find survivors, it is often very dangerous for the rescuers to go into those damaged buildings to offer help. However, robots can bravely charge into these unsafe situations. They are often equipped with tanklike treads or other movement systems that allow them to easily climb over piles of rubble. They might also be equipped with arms to move obstacles, tools to cut open new pathways, or even medical treatments.

If you need certain kinds of surgery, you might be surprised to find out that your doctor will be a robot. These surgical robots are able to perform extremely precise movements. Unlike human surgeons, they do not have to worry about unsteady hands. They can make the smallest possible cuts for each surgery, making it easier for patients to heal afterward. Human doctors give orders to these robots and observe the

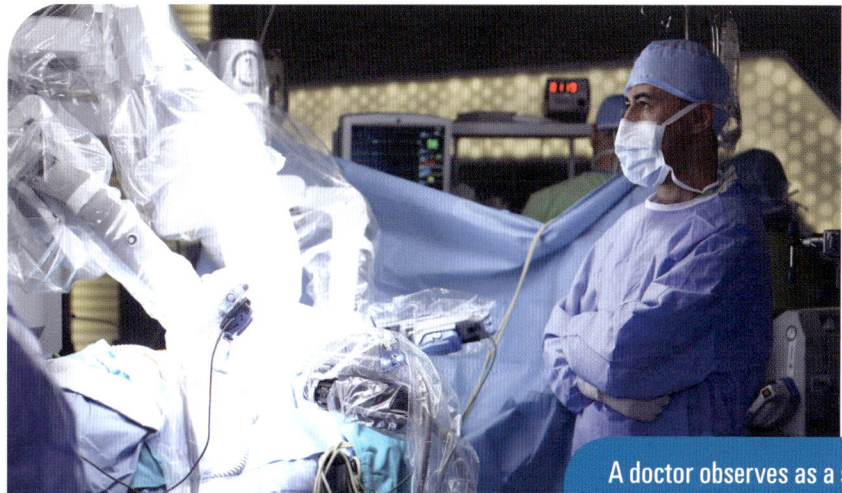

A doctor observes as a surgical robot performs an operation.

EMERGING TECH

Pepper robots await customers at an information stand in a mall in Japan.

procedures. However, inventors are hoping to create surgical robots that don't need any help at all from human doctors.

Even in basic, everyday situations such as shopping or eating at restaurants, robots are becoming a more common sight. For example, a humanoid robot named Pepper is used at many stores in Japan. It understands several languages and can recognize human emotions by reading facial expressions. It is also equipped with a touch screen customers can use. Pepper's job is to greet customers and answer questions they might have as they shop. Robots have also been put to work as waiters at restaurants, and they could soon be seen in many other jobs that involve interacting with people.

EMERGING TECH

Chapter 3

At Home and in the Classroom

Nowadays, it is becoming more common for robots to interact with people in their daily lives. Many people keep robots in their homes to help out with a variety of household tasks. With robots handling the chores, people are freed up to focus their

Robotic vacuum cleaners can be programmed using a simple remote control.

Household robots such as automated lawn mowers can save their owners a great deal of time and effort.

attention on other things. One very popular example of a household robot is Roomba. Roomba is a vacuum cleaner that roams around on its own looking for messes to clean. Not only does this device save time, but it can also vacuum areas that people might not be able to reach with a regular vacuum cleaner. Other household robots can take care of time-consuming tasks such as mowing the lawn or cleaning a swimming pool.

EMERGING TECH

Inside a Robot's "Mind"

A robot's "thinking" is usually controlled by a computer program. This means computer programmers are just as important to the creation of a new robot as the engineers who design robot bodies. These experts use special programming languages to write the **code** that makes up a robot's thinking abilities. The more complicated a robot is, the harder it can be to write code that works correctly. Just as inventors must create prototype robots and keep improving them over time, programmers must constantly test and revise their code. They look for errors called bugs and find ways to fix them. Eventually, if all goes well, the robot's program will work as its creators intended.

Robots can also make good pets. In 1999, Sony introduced a robotic dog named AIBO. Like real dogs, it could play with its owners and learn a variety of tricks. Since then, other robotic pets have hit the market. Many of the latest models even have soft fur and realistic appearances. Robotic pets are a good way for kids to learn the skills they will need to care for real pets. Another common use of these robots is to offer comfort and companionship to sick or elderly people.

You might be surprised one day soon to walk into your classroom on the first day of a new school year to find out that your teacher is a robot. The robot moves around your classroom on wheels. It is equipped with a video screen that shows your human teacher's face.

AIBO robots are programmed to behave much like real dogs.

The real teacher is sitting in front of a computer somewhere else. He might even be located across the world in a distant country. But thanks to the robot, he can see and hear everything that is going on in the classroom as if he were really there. You can ask him questions or get help with your work. Such robots could also connect students to experts who might not normally visit their schools.

If you're really interested in robots, why not try building your own? Many companies offer

EMERGING TECH

Lego Mindstorms is designed to teach kids the skills they need to build and program their own robots.

programmable robot kits and building toys aimed at beginners who want to get started with robot design. One popular example is Lego Mindstorms. This system is based on a programmable robot "brain" and sensors that work along with regular Lego pieces. Users have built robots that can play chess, solve puzzles, play musical instruments, or even build their own Lego creations.

Students who are interested in building robots can enter competitions to show off their incredible creations. At a FIRST Robotics Competition, teams of students build robots that can compete in a variety of games. For example, robots might face off in a basketball-like game that involves throwing balls through hoops or a competition to see which one can stack the tallest tower of objects. First held in 1992, the yearly event has grown rapidly in popularity. In 2016, 75,000 students from 24 countries competed.

Maybe you're more interested in programming a robot's actions instead of building its body. You might try using Sphero or Dash and Dot. These small robots are equipped with lights, speakers, motors, and sensors. You can write programs for them using a tablet or other computer, then load your custom programs into the robots and watch them go. This is a great way to learn about computer programming and find out what robot minds are capable of.

EMERGING TECH

Chapter 4

The Future of Robots

Robots are here to stay. They are only going to become more common as time goes on. If trends continue, they will become less expensive and easier to build. Developments in artificial intelligence, engineering, and materials will make them smarter and more useful than ever before. These improvements will lead to more robots taking over human jobs and more robots being used at home.

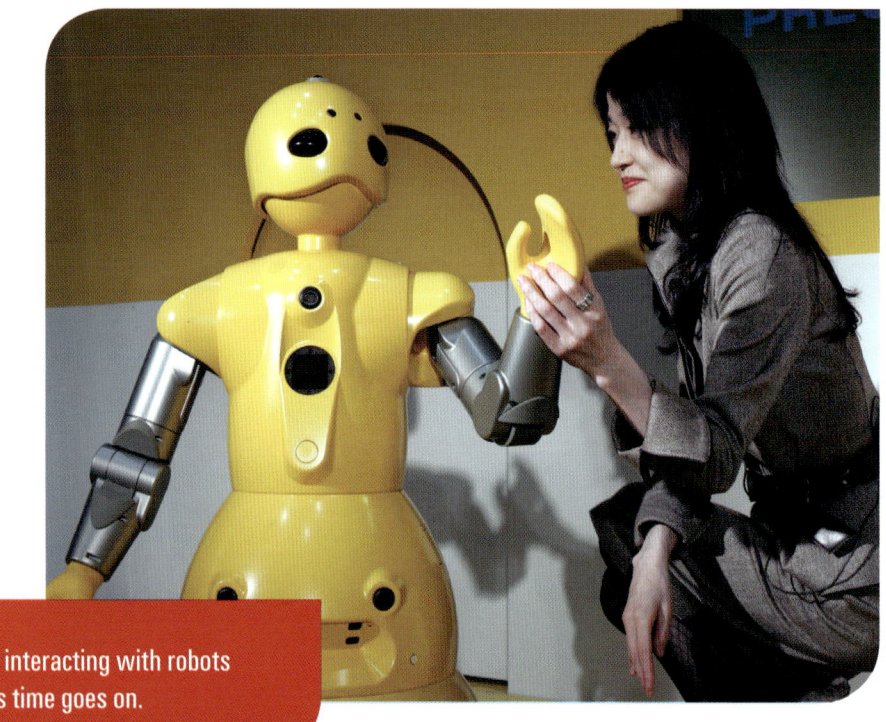

You might find yourself interacting with robots more and more often as time goes on.

ROBOTS

A Google self-driving car cruises on the streets of Mountain View, California.

One major advancement in robotics that is set to make big changes in the world very soon is the self-driving car. Companies such as Google and Tesla and several traditional auto manufacturers are hard at work perfecting fully autonomous vehicles. Many self-driving cars have already taken to the road under test conditions, and the vehicles are expected to be available for public use in the very near future. In fact, one study predicts that up to 10 million of these cars could be on the road by 2020.

EMERGING TECH

Too Much Automation?

There are many reasons for businesses to use robot workers instead of humans. It can be safer, more efficient, and even cheaper to rely on automation. However, there is also a big downside. Every time a business begins using robots in a new job, it takes jobs away from human workers. So far, this has mostly affected factory workers, but it could soon apply to many other jobs, as well. Many truck drivers are expected to lose their jobs as self-driving vehicles take the road. Inventors are also looking for ways to build robots that can work in office jobs.

One recent study predicts that up to 45 percent of all jobs in the United States could be lost to automation in the coming years. Some new jobs will be created to help design, build, and maintain the increasing number of robots. However, this change would still leave many people without any way to make money and support their families. Business and government leaders will need to find ways to solve this issue as robots become more common in the workplace.

Self-driving cars do not need humans to control them. Users simply select a destination, get inside, and relax until they arrive at their destination. The cars use **GPS** technology and a variety of cameras and sensors to keep track of their surroundings and avoid collisions. As these cars begin to replace human-driven cars, they could bring many important benefits. For example, there could be fewer car accidents. Self-driving cars do not commit human errors, such as falling asleep at the wheel or driving distracted. These robotic cars could also reduce

ROBOTS

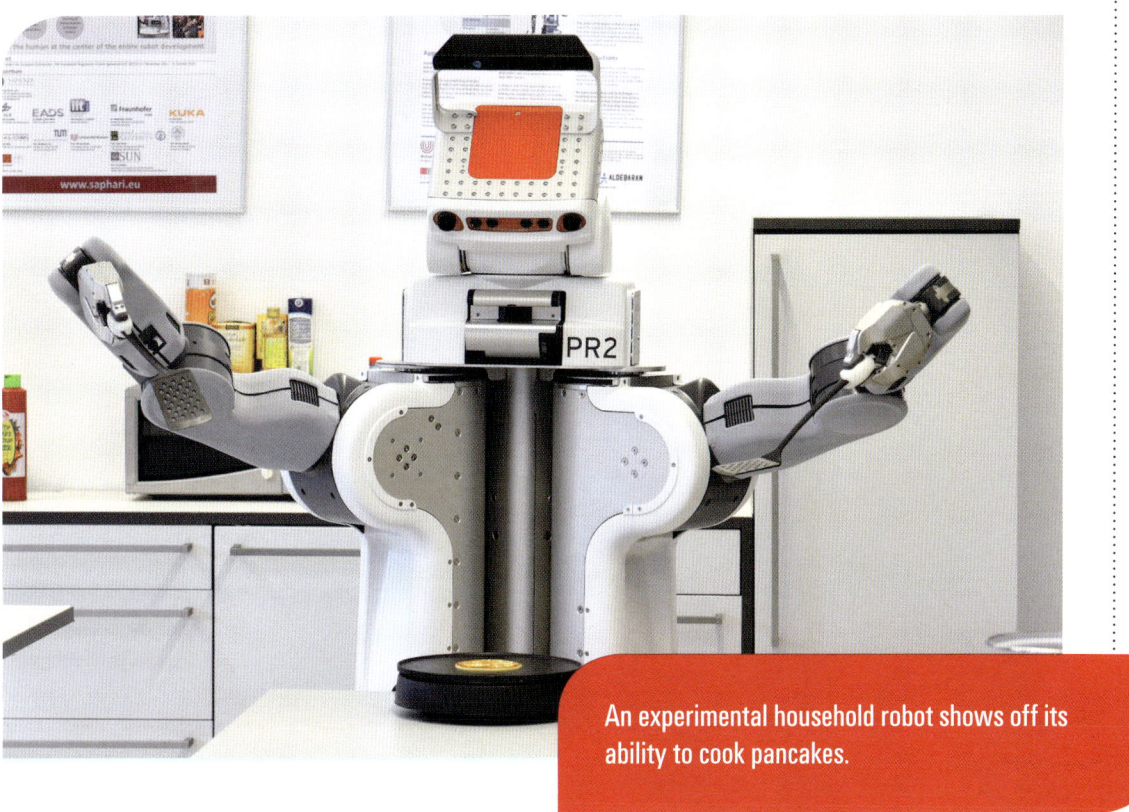

An experimental household robot shows off its ability to cook pancakes.

the need for parking spaces in crowded areas. When people get out of the car at their destination, the car can simply head to an out-of-the-way area and wait for passengers.

It's not hard to see a future where robots play a part in almost all of your daily activities. Imagine waking up for school one morning to the alarm from your household robot maid. You head into the kitchen, where a robot is preparing your breakfast. After you've gotten ready, you use your smartphone to summon a self-driving car that will take you to school.

27

EMERGING TECH

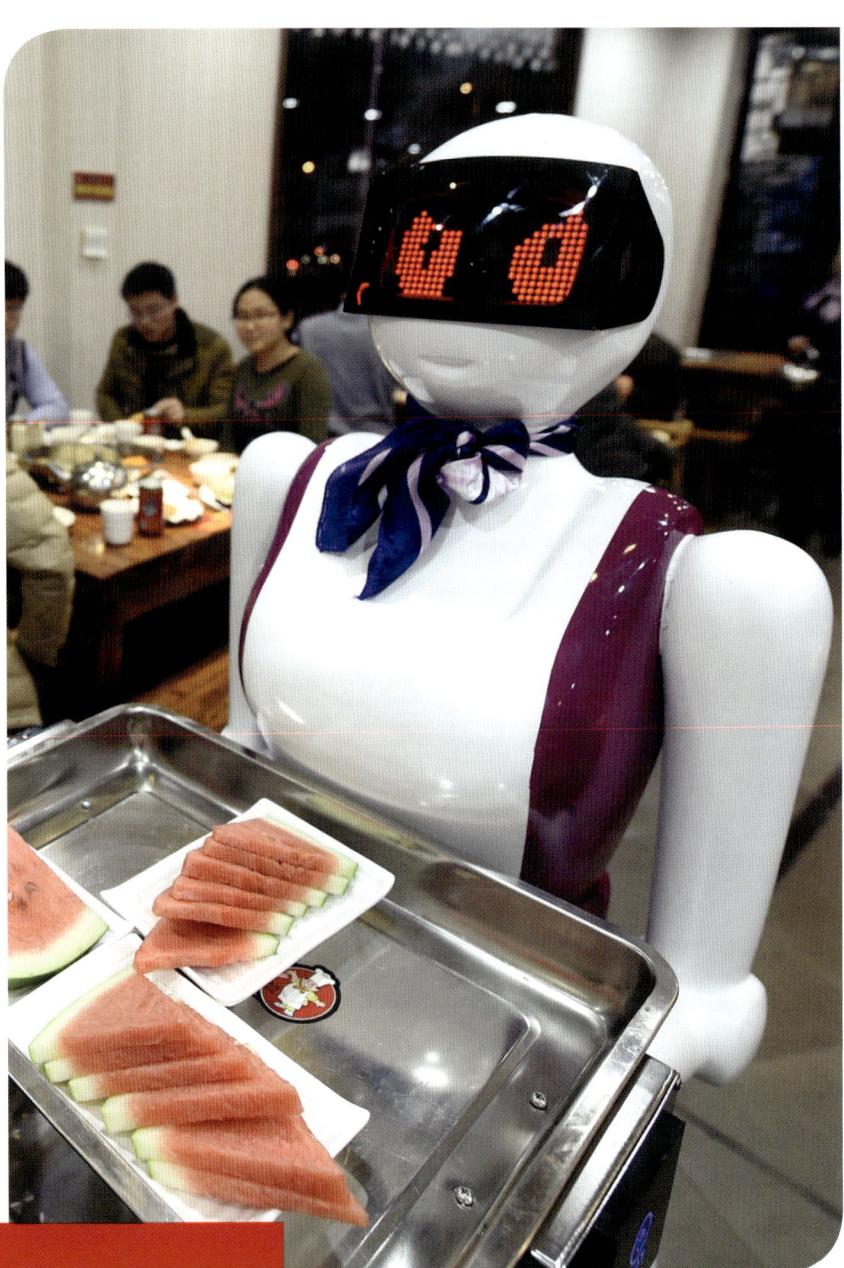

A robot server carries a tray of fruit at a restaurant in China.

At school, you learn from teachers all around the world who connect to your classroom using robots. You also spend some class time working with classmates to build a robot of your own. After school, your mom picks you up in another self-driving car to take you to a doctor's appointment. At the doctor's office, you are greeted by a robot receptionist. A robot nurse measures your height, weight, and blood pressure. Once you're done, you meet up with the rest of your family and head to dinner at a popular new restaurant. The host and waiter are both robots, and they provide excellent service. Even some of the cooking is done by robots.

When you get home, all the housework is already finished. Your family's household robots were hard at work all day. This means everyone has plenty of time to relax in the evening.

As robots become more common, there could be a lot of changes in the way many people live. There could also be surprising new developments that no one has even considered yet. The only thing that's for certain is that we are in for an exciting future. Will you be a part of the robot revolution?

Glossary

autonomous (aw-TAH-nuh-muhs) acting independently

code (KODE) the instructions of a computer program

efficient (ih-FISH-uhnt) working very well and not wasting time or energy

engineers (en-juh-NEERZ) people trained to design and build devices, processes, machines, and other structures

GPS (JEE PEE ESS) a satellite-based system that helps find a location or route to a location; GPS stands for "global positioning system"

humanoid (HYOO-muh-noyd) designed to look like human beings

prototype (PROH-tuh-tipe) the first version of an invention that tests an idea to see if it will work

sensors (SEN-surz) instruments that can detect and measure changes and send the information to a controlling device

simulations (sim-yuh-LAY-shuhnz) trial runs to act out a real event

Find Out More

BOOKS

Crane, Cody. *Robots*. New York: Children's Press, 2018.

Otfinoski, Steven. *Making Robots*. New York: Children's Press, 2016.

WEB SITES

FIRST Robotics Competition
www.firstinspires.org/robotics/frc
Learn more about this popular robot-building competition for students.

Lego Mindstorms
www.lego.com/en-us/mindstorms
Find out more about this popular robot-building kit and check out videos of some of the cool robots people have created with it.

Index

arms, 8–9, 15
artificial intelligence, 6, 24
automatons, 8

classroom robots, 20–21, 29
communication, 5, 9, 17
competitions, 22–23

designs, 5, 12, 26
Devol, George, 8–9

exploration robots, 11–12

factory robots, 6, 9, 11, 26

household robots, 18–19, 27, 29

law enforcement robots, 12
lawn-mowing robots, 19
learning, 6, 20

medical robots, 15, 17, 29
military robots, 12–13
movement, 5, 8, 10, 12, 14–15, 20

ocean exploration, 11
office robots, 6–7, 26, 29

pet robots, 20
programming, 5–6, 7, 20, 22, 23

rescue robots, 14–15
rovers, 11

security robots, 6–7
self-driving vehicles, 25–27, 29
sensors, 6, 7, 11, 22, 23, 26
service robots, 17, 29
stand-in robots, 20–21, 29

About the Author

Josh Gregory is the author of more than 100 books for kids. He has written about everything from animals to technology to history. A graduate of the University of Missouri-Columbia, he currently lives in Portland, Oregon.

629.892 G
Gregory, Josh,
Robots /

FLT

09/17